CREAM PAGES

THE DIALOGUES OF

TANIA KOSWYCZ
& RICHARD LAYZELL

First published in 2008 by ResCen Publications

Editor: Joshua Sofaer

ISBN 978 0955059148

This book was realised with the support of the Live Art Development Agency and Middlesex University.

ResCen
The Centre for Research into Creation in the Performing Arts
Middlesex University
Trent Park
Bramley Road
London N14 4YZ

www.rescen.net

CONTENTS

11 DECEMBER 07
FARRINGDON, LONDON

RICHARD LAYZELL We're through.

TANIA KOSWYCZ Don't be ridiculous.

RL No, with *Cream Pages*, I mean.

TK I wouldn't count on it. I can see the need for an additional printed Intro for every showing of *The Manifestation*.

RL You don't think this is enough?

TK Of course our audience will understand that this slim volume gives them all the background they need, but a few site-specific words on a separate sheet will make the ideal apéritif.

RL *Cream Pages* isn't only supposed to act as an introduction to *The Manifestation*.

TK Who says?

RL Our publishers.

TK Fuck the publishers. I didn't say that, they're lovely. And we're in a preface of substance here. Make no mistake, this book is totally stand alone. Agreed?

RL Absolutely.

20 OCTOBER 07
CROUCH END, LONDON

TK You sound weird.

RL I feel shattered. Think it's partly the stress of working towards *The Manifestation*. It's looming.

TK Pressure is telling. You're wanting to pin it to the wall already. This is the mere work-in-progress. First venue not till February in Glasgow. You're out of control.

RL Maybe. But it's also the anxiety of hoping that *The Perfect Image* will be truthful to our collaboration and successfully feed into *The Manifestation*.

TK It's one potential element. Why get hung up when there's *Falling Phoebe* and *The Stumbling Block* in the wings for Glasgow?

RL I guess.

TK There's more to it. Surely this has to do with going public. Equal billing. Names in print at last. And we were limited here to photography, to *The Perfect Image*.

RL Which was no bad thing, as it turned out.

TK No bad thing? What an understatement. This is a sharp installation, a triptych of fragmented vignettes.

RL It gets a bit lost in the documentation photos.

TK What does?

RL The installation.

TK It would do. It's a perspectival challenge and your images are crap. Either you or your camera is not up to the job. See if Kel's available to take this on. I want some decent documentation.

RL OK, OK.

TK Incorporating the dialogue was the thing.

RL For sure. It's such a relief to find a form for it, even though people tend to read this piece from right to left.

TK Visual literacy, or textual illiteracy.

RL I think they enter into the space from the door opening, so that's right to left. Hadn't thought of that.

TK We didn't discuss it, you mean.

RL The five floor pieces become illusory holes in the material fabric, and they're repeatable, like the postcards.

TK There you go with the 'repeatable'. Yes, they could become part of *The Manifestation* but equally they may not. Cool it. Order yourself a green tea. Finally we're in full collaboration and you lose it. Don't go running scared now that my voice is finally heard.

RL I guess I'm in some shock, Tania. I haven't experienced the intensity of building an installation in an exhibition space for some time. It takes longer than I remembered.

TK And my influence?

RL Hats off, Tania. That was the biggest shock.

TK How fucking patronising.

RL Collaboration is a complex business.

TK Bollocks. I'm all good news. What have we learnt here?

RL What do you think?

TK Trust would be nice, but sounds like it's a way off. That the underlying concept of *The Manifestation* and *The Dialogue* is sound. That people engage with the postcard piece as a concise, snappy and accessible format. That there's quality and clarity here. That they get it. That it's about fucking time this project kicked off. And we have SVA to thank. How about you?

RL You've covered quite a bit there. For me the wall piece became a major project. I'm a bit confused about asking Kiera to be your postcard scribe.

TK Why?

RL Because she's not you. Because some people thought I'd written the whole thing.

TK That bothers me. Kiera doesn't. Anything else?

RL I can imagine the floor pieces becoming localised: local images, local soil, with some larger ones. I feel more confident. People seemed to engage with it.

TK Excuse me, it's terrific. The whole fucking thing is fabulous. That's what you're struggling with, success. It's a triumph. You surprised yourself. Bring on *Cream Pages*.

RL You have any thoughts about that by the way?

TK At last you ask. The title's hitting the spot. Me to thank for that. You're panicking. It's OK to leave stuff out. Need the global reach. Forget the external viewpoint.

RL How do you mean?

TK The one you're trying to please. Don't leave me to be the sharp shooter.

RL Reverse chronology?

TK Your idea?

RL I think so.

TK Worth hanging on to for now.

RL I guess it's starting to influence what goes in.

TK Just get on and do it. Talk to me more about it. Phil and Joshua, great team.

RL Preface?

TK I don't think we need one. We can just start with the most recent dialogue.

12 OCTOBER 07
STROUD, GLOUCESTERSHIRE

RL I don't want to lose sight of the bigger project. What are we wanting here?

TK This is about producing material that can potentially be used in *The Manifestation* unless I'm on a new novel. So how do current plans feed in?

RL If I'm honest it's only the soil stuff. What about *The Perfect Image*?

TK *The Perfect Image* is all fine and well, but I need convincing that we could show these SVA images on our tour.

RL What about the strip of postcard-sized images? Or the very large ones? So what are we missing out here?

TK Hello, yes, I am receiving you. Glad to be consulted finally. Of course I don't know how the whole of *The Manifestation* will fit together but this all seems a bit safe playing to me. There are plenty of people out there toying with the photographic image, you know what I'm saying. But our perfection will be different. I see video stills as holding potential status.

RL Might be useful to sum up what's been going on with this photographic stuff.

TK Be my guest.

RL We first started talking consciously about image-making in Thailand and that was related to SVA. It was about the detail, the everyday, the perceptual focus, the re-contextualising, the elevating, the studio as place of research, the process, the materials and materiality. In Asia it became about universality and was integrated into our dialogues. What strikes me is that it's not so much to do with photography as process.

TK It's all bollocks unless you feel the pressure from me.

RL If it recedes then this is more about image, still image and the dialogue. Yes, I remember now, how originally we thought we'd include the dialogue in with the photos.

TK Well, well, if you think you've got it ask me. There's a long way to go. I like the look but not the substance. Keep trying.

RL You got inside my psyche here in Stroud and I didn't know till we were straight talking in Thailand. Like we were already doing it.

TK Your illicit camera from the company crash coming out to play half-serious shit surprises us all. We have a relationship on our hands.

RL It's a case in point, the lens has been my screen scene not even a reflex action. This looking down and in. A stack of stuff shifting your axis.

TK Dust and detritus get me out of here. Rather swim with a cockroach than a woodlouse. Outside space coming in. You never told me the nightclub burnt down, hot stuff.

RL You get my text? Post is fucked.

TK Why not steal in a couple of images from Thailand – it was all happening at roughly the same time. Will you notice?

RL This is hard hand writing ahead of the game. The space of hanging is a different frame. But there's another way to navigate, like stand alone fragments.

TK I'd like to evaluate my contribution to the whole project. Relax, joking. We've moved on, sure sure.

RL You chose the big ones, can I have a free hand with the postcards?

TK No point scoring, you agreed with my choice. You're not running off into full-on 'who's the control freak' now. It's not happening. Words are even, images too.

RL We need more attention. This has been the basis. Check it out. Stake a claim. Simon knew the score. Temperature readings were the first fly on the wall.

TK We were talking before and after. An opportunity for spearing in the depths. I'm OK, you're OK. My foot in your hard hat. And the builders noticed.

RL Let's get image specific.

TK I thought we already were. OK then: Dark warm ruffled fold-up seeks sharp pit spat on top of the world. Send photo.

RL Whose hammer head tells the script? The table gets the pressure. It ain't begun. Damnation. Glory.

TK Screw your silver side of warm exterior. This vertical slash opens up a crack in my world. Cover up quick before a stray hand stabs my sublimation.

RL As if size matters. We're on the shelf of destiny here. The ink is a speaking circuit. It's on the cards.

TK The blues sit back and take it. You come, you go. Still hanging even if you smother me with the crisp clean brilliance of white from home base around the kitchen table. Aren't we nice.

RL The gutter bleeds success. A rash of stale spice.

TK If you think this trio was my choice you've gotta be fucking joking. It's all yours my friend I don't sport pink nowhere, another mistake.

RL Hats off to the money makers, raisers and seepers. You drag out the dry dirt so we can *Beddin*.

TK We need to establish a pricing structure. Is this a series of individual saleable pieces or one? You onto this?

RL It's a one piece one-off.

TK You need to get a black suit. You thought about the opening? I want full representation. Go for profile.

RL I'm ready for a declaration of intent. Perfection isn't a half of it.

27 SEPTEMBER 07
SPIKE ISLAND, BRISTOL

TK So?

RL A follow up.

TK Is this an open dialogue to The Associates?

RL Yes. A proposition is the way to go, you know.

TK I'm winding you up.

RL So?

TK Me?

RL Yes.

TK I can see the potential now.

RL Like?

TK Curatorial intent, collaboration as part of the process, a space of opportunity, *The Manifestation* as a proposition and installation.

RL Not quite sure what you mean.

TK Wake up Richard, think of the possibilities: this could be linked to *White on White* or *The Table as Metaphorical Space*, not to mention the connection with studio practice.

RL But The Associates don't strictly have studios.

TK Hello, are you receiving me? That's the point. You were talking to them about how you work in cafes or wherever. Like asking the 'What is a studio?' question. That can be a key aspect of this piece. It can be partly about creating a 'social space' within the gallery.

RL Like Kath is talking about for the new Firstsite?

TK Yes and more so. The installation could be about integrating temporary workspaces as tables or table forms. The visitor can join in, sit and participate. The Spike Island café can be involved.

RL Like exploring the nature of working, thinking, studio and all that?

TK Absolutely.

RL I guess it could go beyond Spike to some kind of intervention with certain Bristol cafes, along the lines of what happened in Lillehammer, when rain closed play at the Park Caffeen and I wandered the streets as town waiter, café to café.

TK Mmm. I can feel some press interest coming on. Were we talking back then?

RL Not strictly speaking. You were around but we didn't go public until September 03 in Australia. You must have been in the ether though.

TK Don't give me this stuff. Whose ether is whose? Really. They could see that.

RL Who?

TK The Associates.

RL You up for this then?

TK Sure. I'm in the thick of it. You haven't asked how *White on White* would fit in.

RL Oh, I thought it was obvious.

TK Go on then.

RL I imagine you're thinking of this as a large installation where *The Table as Metaphorical Space* is a key element but there will be others, like our dialogues and *White on White* for example. So an area could be devoted to a physical representation of the nature and physicality of painting white on white within an architectural context.

TK Worthy effort. Help yourself to a muesli bar. How about you?

RL Me?

TK Any ideas or propositions?

RL Well, strangely enough, I was also wondering about recreating *The Studio Project* in some way, allocating each artist a public studio space-as-show. We'd show *The Manifestation* in an adjoining space, or part of the space.

TK So we're on similar lines here. How about dates?

RL I think this is the beginning of a dialogue.

TK Keep it real. If this is gonna happen it's better for all concerned to have a potential schedule of some kind.

RL Sure. Can I give out your email address?

TK Who to?

RL The Associates.

TK OK but I can't always guarantee replying.

RL I can though.

TK You don't always reply to me.

5 FEBRUARY 07
DUNDEE CONTEMPORARY ARTS, TAYSIDE

TK Who paid for the coffees?

RL They were on the house.

TK Who signed for them?

RL Clive.

TK You miss a trick there? Where was the compelling act of generosity? And where was my formal representation? You didn't even open your laptop.

RL This was a different kind of meeting and I went with the flow.

TK Actually I thought you did OK. Nice segue from 'how's it going Clive' to 'this is *The Manifestation*' and 'what do you say?'

RL As this was our twelfth meeting with curators I thought we could risk a new format. You must have been represented enough or he wouldn't have made his big suggestion.

TK That we could curate other artists into it?

RL Yes, a different guest artist at each venue maybe ... or a work of local relevance, like a William Burges object or something from the Victor Batte-Lay collection in Colchester, so it could be historical or of course a contemporary artist we take a shine to ...

TK Was this interesting, collaborative, or a side track?

RL You tell me.

TK It was the beginning of a relationship. Full marks to him. You're on a B minus. My hesitation is that he was deferring to the appointment of a new curator and may have no say as the story unfolds. But, for me, this was a result.

RL You like the gallery spaces at DCA?

TK Sure. We're likely starting off in Glasgow, why not take in Dundee further along the road? It houses the most successful bar in the city. That speaks to me.

RL He had other questions.

TK Remind me.

RL Like how to make it accessible to a general audience.

TK As if this isn't already your ongoing obsession. He's losing points on this one. Get me out of here I need a cigarette.

RL Perhaps he didn't realise that we're in the thick of that particular debate.

TK Maybe you were the person to take this on at the time. The work tells the story, Richard. We are a beacon of wonder. The people will know and understand. I speak the truth.

RL He also asked if we'd go ahead with the tour anyway.

TK Without the funding pending?

RL Yes, and when I thought about it, it seemed like we most likely would. Am I right?

TK Absolutely, I've waited long enough for this to be oven-ready. I'd expect you to join me on the late shift at The Elbow Room if we're short on cash investment. You may not get the opportunity to work with me again, so don't blow it 'cos of the fear factor. You reading my lines? Backing off?

RL I hear you.

15 NOVEMBER 06
BLUECOAT, LIVERPOOL

RL What was your take?

TK Delightful.

RL Really?

TK Venue was a little strange, like we were projecting our wares onto a bathroom wall with the door open.

RL This was Out of the Bluecoat during their rebuild.

TK No need to state the obvious, I'm saying it was hard to get a feel of the spaces in the new building, sitting around a table in a Liverpool tiling showroom.

RL I don't think we actually talked much about those specifics.

TK That might just be my point. You were so infatuated by setting up the data projector and the seductive chocolate biscuits that you skated too light on core issues.

RL I think we got drawn into some local politics, like how we'd be talking to Lewis at the Biennial the next day.

TK Why mention it, trying to impress? Leave that to me. I'm impressive without name-dropping. You allowed for deflection on this one. What would Lewis say and all that. You got a bit thrown by Bryan chewing on a specific vision of *The Manifestation* and spent too long on our history.

RL It's true, I do sometimes struggle with the 'what will it look like?' question.

TK Why?

RL Because it's a reasonable enough request. I put myself in their shoes and think, yep, what are we talking about here?

TK Pathetic. Get a grip. Empathy is your downfall. I thought you were over this one. These meetings are about putting across *The Manifestation* and our collaboration as an entire package, with the dialogue as core framework.

RL Maybe I was thrown by not having met Sara before, that she'd recently arrived from Texas, that we were sitting around the table with our coats on. Denver it wasn't.

TK That's in Colorado.

RL You know what I mean.

TK Now and then. It was definitely the tiles. Anyway I thought they were great.

RL Who?

TK Bryan and Sara. Especially when Bryan asked how it would be if a curator wanted to work with me solo.

RL How would you feel about this?

TK What do you think? Job done.

RL But I'd want to be credited. And I thought we'd ruled this possibility out when we first started talking.

TK Well well, not my recollection at all.

25 MAY 06
SPACE, HACKNEY, LONDON

TK Good lobby.

RL Brand new apparently.

TK Nice gallery space, quality wooden floor.

RL Like a free space.

TK Social space almost.

RL By default.

TK Surprised?

RL Am a bit drawn to it.

TK Seriously?

RL Aren't you?

TK Yes, but not seriously, no profile.

RL You should have said.

TK You didn't ask.

RL The meeting?

TK I wasn't sure about being represented as a bottle of wine.

RL Argentinian.

TK From Benfleet in Essex, come on ...

RL I thought it worked well, made an assertive point.

TK George?

RL Seemed a bit phased.

TK Because Anna brought him in, as curator, mid-stream. This could happen again, we'll have to build in the eventuality. You and Anna seemed to hit it off.

RL It was good to see her.

TK So what's the connection, remind me?

RL She became the curator at Kettles Yard while I was in the middle of *The Revolution – You're In It*. We often seem to speak on the same panels. She wrote an essay for *Enhanced Performance*. She worked on the curating course at Goldsmiths. I wrote a piece for an issue of *Art and Design* she was editing.

TK That's a bunch of stuff. Where do I fit in?

RL You're not really asking that.

TK I did feel acknowledged. But what are we doing here?

RL Space is a significant artists' resource. Anna knows me. She's well connected.

TK Hm. Good location, I grant you. Hackney Wick would be better. Your scene historically. May not be the kind of support I'm looking for, need to consider my emerging profile, but could benefit from her curatorial experience.

RL It went somewhere. We hadn't actually gone there looking for a show. To me this felt like a work for the first time, like the meeting itself was almost enough.

TK For?

RL As a part of the process, like we'd discussed.

TK And the context?

RL For me there's a compelling link with the studio as metaphor and a link with our origins. Space was formed by artists for artists.

TK OK, not ruling anything out. Just don't get deflected.

21 AUGUST 06
PENZANCE, CORNWALL

RL Doubting anchor footage can't be the only reason.

TK Out of schedule, drawn to keep it going. Or find the essence of excrescence.

RL Boot stacked, curvers bent, traffic jammed, rain break, no rush, pleasure of the real thing.

TK Location scout. Harbour or war memorial.

RL Harbour.

TK Harbour. Nice framing.

RL Camera discretion. Harbour wall. Could be shooting boats, would be.

TK If you only knew.

RL That box, chalked up and ready, raising the patina of blue framed by weather rust. Angular repetition one two one three. Coming up nicely.

TK Square in the circle.

RL Tide's out, horizon radiates.

TK Ship's in. We're out.

17 AUGUST 06
PENZANCE, CORNWALL

RL Weather forecast is bloody awful.

TK Don't over-react. Do the quiet stuff this afternoon in the rain.

RL How's it looking?

TK Like there are plenty of distractions.

RL Only being sociable and responsive.

TK Don't give me the flannel. Remember why you're here.

RL What about not needing to 'work' all the time?

TK Sure. This ain't Norway 03. It's Penzance 06. Inclement weather, you're the only suit in the street, pirate 'n' chips and we're talking.

RL What do you think about cleaning that yellow-suited fisherman mannequin clenching the blue fish tail?

TK No dirt. Too cute. Pubs?

RL Not yet. Bit early.

TK You can see it working?

RL I can see the 'working' working. Can you?

TK Always did.

RL Shall we talk about Saturday evening?

TK Not yet. Enough on. Focus for Christ's sake.
Make a list:
swimming hats and costumes
blue paint
step ladder
sort music
see the pool
meet the café people ...

RL Cloth for cleaning, graph paper for *Curve Measuring* ... schedule for tomorrow?

TK How about three shifts:
10·00 – 12·00
13·00 – 15·00
15·30 – 17·00
17·30 – tech at the pool.
What about a context for the gardening?

RL I brought some tools.

TK Something that matches your suited image, like a large wicker basket.

RL Good idea. I'll head off then. Causewayhead and the pool.

* * *

TK You're back then. I thought we were in some kind of equal collaboration now.

RL We are.

TK Why am I not credited in the publicity then?

RL I thought you were.

TK Why am I feeling excluded?

RL Are you?

TK Yes. Think about it.

RL I am. It's your aesthetic of absence. It's my visibility.

TK You're making excuses. This piece, *The Radiant Curve*, is my work as well as yours. Bring on equal billing, that will shake you out of it.

RL Of what?

TK Your self-importance. Your reluctance to give me space. Anyway, nice basket.

RL Thanks. Glad you approve. Thought I'd lost one of the small curve-measurers en route.

TK Oh dear.

RL I got a bit obsessive about it. Better to have four than three, for symmetry.

TK Who says we need symmetry?

RL I went back to the store where I'd bought the basket, looking for it, but no luck. Then, coming down the hill, man in the art shop tapped on the window and came out clutching it.

TK Quality small town service or business is pretty slow. Good reflection on the thing itself, just a piece of wood isn't it?

RL Birch ply. That's what gives them 'spring back'. And the toggles add a professional touch. Not so sure about the green nylon fishing string from Ban Phe.

TK A colour issue. But let's revel in these choice connections of design consistency. And we were talking in Thailand. How's it looking in the pool?

RL Fine. Not quite how I remembered it. The Jubilee Pool. Serious swimmers in there. It's enormous. Abundance of radiant curves. Borough engineer Captain F Latham excelled himself. Holly, the Head Lifeguard, very easy-going. Rebecca in the café will be my supervisor. Be great to paint *White on White* or *Blue on Blue* in there. Easy pickings in the Pool Café.

TK Don't get smug. This 'permission' stuff is all very well but the edge is sharper when you simply turn up and brush. Just keep sporting the Venetian pirate tie. Didn't we buy it on the very first day of *International Cleaning* in St Mark's Square?

RL Hey, you could be right.

TK You going social tonight or re-working the playlist for Saturday?

RL Hoping to do both. There's a gathering. Good to meet up with the other artists and catch up with the press interest in Kira and animal rights. Newlyn Art Gallery under pressure. All hands on deck. Be nice if you could come along.

TK Not my frame of reference as you well know. Anyway don't lose the plot. We start work for real tomorrow. Speak after breakfast.

11 MAY 05
PIOTRKOW TRYBUNALSKI, POLAND

RL Intriguing items in a shop window en route from problematic lodgings. Not opening till 9am, so another kind of window opens up, allowing for a few ground-focussed photos around the old town.

TK Is this becoming another global project?

RL The ground photo? Possibly, but hard to eclipse the Thai series.

TK Or the SVA details. You're cramming it in trying to do the right thing again. Enough going on. You don't listen.

RL It is looking like a pretty busy day, maybe you're right:
09·00 Breakfast at the restaurant in town. Anne Bean arrives. We chat over hard egg soft bread
10·00 To Europa for materials, technical briefings, translation and assistant possibilities
11.30 All international artists meet at Europa for walk to:
12·00 Inaugural ceremony of Academy of Performance Art at the Piotrkow Trybunalski Museum
13·00 Europa for technical and space set-up, translation briefings
15·00 Begin street interventions
17·00 Technical set-up part two and the evening programme for Interakcje Day 3 begins
19·00–20·00 Our performance

TK What did you decide to have translated?

RL YOU MADE ME DO IT /
TANIA KOSWYCZ ARTIST AND FRIEND /
YOU ARE ABSENT /
I'M NOT HERE /

RASHNA, DAVID, KEVIN AND TANIA /
YOU TOLD ME TO WALK IN CIRCLES AND READ /
YOU TOLD ME TO HIT THE STATUE /
YOU TOLD ME TO DECORATE THE MOTORBIKE

TK I've got some comments about my representation.

RL I can imagine, but can't it wait till we reflect on the whole event?

TK You mean I might feel differently?

RL I mean this is only part of how you were represented.

TK I would hope so. Hold on a minute. Why wasn't I involved in the translation process? And that text – come on, I don't tell you to 'do' things, that's your take. I sound like a loser. And why bring Rashna and the others into it? Misrepresenting me in Poland of all places. Unbelievable. I know you're under pressure, but this is not happening again, no way. It's a fucking insult, Richard.

RL Who's over-reacting now? Can we get back to the practicals, take some heat out of it?

TK You're gonna tell me anyway so you may as well get on with it.

RL I think we talked about the stuff I'd be bringing over.

TK Dream on.

RL I'm sure we did. So here's the list:
paintbrushes and red fly swat from Greece
OHP slides of you and your work
videotape of Lillehammer
    with three Skyros sequences
Sophocles book
suit and tie
cameras

Interakcje to provide:
video projector
OHP
round table and white cloth
stepladder for outside work
white emulsion paint
bucket and cloths
A3 paper for translation texts
tripod

TK Charming details but I'm not grasping the grit. What happened actually?

RL What happened when?

TK At the ceremony for a start.

RL Jan, who I'd met on the bus from Warsaw, is wearing an ermine gown and a tri-cornered hat. It all seems very official. Local TV are there, including a sound recordist wearing a pink coat, who reminds me of you.

TK Can you really see me in a pink coat?

RL Maybe it was the snakeskin pointed shoes.

TK Please.

RL You'll have to see her photo.

TK I can hardly wait.

RL Anyway, her body language is all wrong, too submissive, not you at all. There's a long wooden table with most of the senior Polish artists sitting behind it. We, the international artists and others, are audience. It goes on. Speech after speech. Official documents are awarded and exchanged. Then we're told to expect a long concluding address in Polish and that will be the end of it. I'm prepared for an intervention and this is the moment.

TK Prepared?

RL I'm wearing black suit, carrying white paint. Walls of the museum are white. There are patches around the doorways in this chamber that need attention. So I get up and get on, during the long speech.

TK You get on with a spontaneous *White on White*?

RL I thought you'd approve of this blatant opportunism, *White on White*, with long handled brush from Skyros.

TK How long?

RL Brush or brushing?

TK Brushing.

RL No idea. Ten or fifteen minutes? I'm a bit hesitant, not wanting to fully undermine the event, but underline it.

TK Security?

RL The museum guard checks me out almost immediately but seems amenable. I mean, what can he say, I'm making improvements.

TK He could stop you.

RL But I look like a professional. And I've started now. I'm working. This one not documented by me.

TK Deliberately?

RL Yes.

TK Ivan would be thrilled.

RL This was *White on White* and *International Cleaning* for Ivan's delectation, action first.

TK I won't get to see the evidence.

RL True. But you get the picture.

TK How did it go down?

RL Plenty of interest from the Poles. But later I begin to doubt the status of the whole event. People tell me the ceremony was a performance in itself. Was there really an academy? If so, this was subtle and we 'international artists' were hoodwinked. Me too, even by staging this.

TK So you wouldn't have gone ahead if you'd realised it was a performance.

RL Probably not. Edge lost.

TK Edge culture. We'll return to this.

RL OK. Back at Europa I'm expecting Gordian, the Polish curator, but he's gone off to get a large block of ice for Paul, a fellow Canadian.

TK I know you have Canadian tendencies but this is going too far.

RL A typo in the daily bulletin. At least my name's spelt right. Dundee room-mate Kevin Henderson becomes Kewin Shenderson. And he's about to start outside a very slow six-hour shuffle based on Beckett's stage notes for Endgame. The promise of a technical run-through for me is evaporating, along with my command of Polish, but I do now have an assistant, Magdalena. She's 16 but looks about 12, although she seems to know the whole town. And Interakcje is big news for Piotrkow Trybunalski, rated third in their hierarchy of tourist attractions, which of course appeals to me.

TK The libertarian's social conscience kicks in again.

RL I thought you'd see the PR opportunity.

TK In rural Poland? Please.

RL I ask Magdalena to keep an eye on the video camera as I retouch the gate pillars of a Catholic compound.

TK The camera's back then.

RL It's discreetly placed. We'd lack the record, it's as simple as that.

TK Is it?

RL No. It's different with a camera. But the balance has shifted. The durational is more authentic.

TK How would it be if I was on camera?

RL I don't know ... great, I think.

TK I might start to direct you.

RL Perhaps I need it. Maybe I don't.

TK Are you csik or spill?

RL Definitely csik at the road sign. It starts to flow. Stepladder has failed to materialise so I start to balletically chuck the damp cloth at the top sign. Movements become gestural. Repetitions become cyclical. Traffic flows around me. The signs can't get much cleaner. They're actually rusty on close inspection. I begin to paint the edges of the bottom sign, to Warszawa. Not a perfect colour match but signage is enhanced. I become more aware of the patina of the rust, and start to question my actions. How would this have been received in Soviet times?

TK Sounds like you're losing your judgement.

RL How can you tell?

TK Intuition. Reading between the lines.

RL It's a great dynamic though, I'm not complaining, it's achieving what I'd hoped for, a development of *International Cleaning*. I'm in Ivan's space, the camera forgotten.

TK So, is it a performance?

RL I don't know any more. I have a function. I'm in a public space, being useful.

TK And a foil to Europa later on.

RL I've lost touch with that. This is all there is. But, now you mention it, there's a shadow here. I'll be painting *White on White* in front of an expectant seated audience, in the context of performance art.

Here there is the interplay with social function, even urban regeneration.

TK Careful. I don't imagine they use that particular terminology in the land of my fathers.

RL I thought your parents came from the Czech Republic.

TK Western Poland, near the border, place called Jelenia Góra. Prague is closer than Warsaw.

RL You been back?

TK A few times since it opened up. Relatives. Potatoes in many guises. Woods. Midges. Teenagers wanting to know about the West, smoking fags called West. Thank Christ I'm second generation out-of-here.

RL I like it, there's a kind of enthusiasm and innocence that we've lost. Look at the numbers in the audience here for example.

TK Where?

RL At Europa.

TK Have you started then?

RL Yes. I'm painting out the patches on the wall we'll be projecting onto. There's no technical set-up time at all. It happens, after a fashion, with the audience sitting there.

TK Your choice to get involved with this fracas.

RL You said it. This is a festival where the programming happens the day before. I'm fortunate to have a projector at all, and they almost abandon trying to assemble the OHP.

TK Csik?

RL I try to make this set-up in near darkness appear seamless and intentional but it's too tall an order. The Lillehammer video, *You Made Me Do It*, begins. Still-wet white paint gleams in the projected light.

I interact with the circular table, replicating some video moments.

TK You wearing the same striped shirt?

RL No, but there are three shirts in the video, although you're right, would have been better to wear the striped one. This is the fourth or fifth performance this evening, not an ideal slot. It's beginning to have the intensity of the NRLA. A highlight is showing a video clip of that afternoon's street actions, fresh and local.

TK Translations? How am I manifested?

RL By Sarah's lime green raincoat. I drape it over the back of a chair and refer to it now and again.

TK I can live with that. I hope you got permission. Is this piece called *Talking to Tania* again?

RL Yes.

TK Confusing, I don't remember agreeing to this. Do they get the subtleties of our relationship?

RL This is the big challenge as there's so little English spoken.

TK Could be an advantage. No chance of you going overdrive on the OHPs. Some clarity for a change.

RL The translated words, read out by Zofia, a new assistant, cover some of the ground. I ask some Polish audience members at the end what they make of our relationship and they recognise how we talk, who we are.

TK Not disastrous then. Me?

RL I think you come out of it pretty well.

TK Communication?

RL I contact you a few times, especially at the point of ending. You tell me to take some space and not go for the obvious. I combine gesture, timing and white paint with the Sophocles book, ending with a hand-print on the cover. Thanks.

TK Don't thank me, we're in this together.

8 MAY 05
WARSAW TO PIOTRKOW TRYBUNALSKI, POLAND

TK Hey, what's up, thought you were off air.

RL Stuff to talk about.

TK Where are you for Christ's sake?

RL Careful, this is the land of the now very venerated late Pope.

TK Whereabouts?

RL Warsaw, on the way to Piotrkow Trybunalski for a performance festival called Interakcje. Had you forgotten?

TK Been busy. Hadn't registered. Am I in this?

RL Absolutely, but it's a bit macho and intense, very East European, not really your scene.

TK Remember my roots. Why are we doing it?

RL It was an opportunity, you know the score, and not my first time in Poland. I like the relaxed interface between art and theatre here.

TK Are you sure it's so relaxed? I don't recall this particular happy muesli.

RL Now that you mention it, man with a ponytail just came up to me and described my performance in Minsk six years ago as 'theatrical'.

TK So what's the difference?

RL This dark, intense, durational, action-based tradition.

TK Soviet reflex. They need to let it go. Check out the younger generation. They'll be up for it.

RL We just stopped at a social housing complex on the outskirts of Warsaw to visit a gallery in a basement of one of the blocks, and there it all is: an office full of bearded men drinking apple juice laced with vodka, along with a strange assortment of accompaniments including several plates of bendy shaped Wotsits look-alikes. On entering the gallery young documenters wield still and movie cameras and an older man sporadically writes a line of numbers on the wall. I'm greeted by Victor Petrov from Belarus, co-curator of the Navinki performance festival. Haven't seen him since 1999. The inevitable collapse into pigeon communication begins, 'Reechard' ... pause ... 'Victor' ... pause, shrug ... etc. Jan, a founder of this seven year old festival, and quite frail, looks up at me and says quite distinctly 'it's gonna be alright'.

TK I wouldn't trust that. Read the opposite.

RL I wondered if I'd misheard him. But that's the attitude here, it's a very particular ambience, different even from Belarus. This festival will make itself, no set schedule, just ask for what you want. But we're not there yet, this is the taster.

TK You stressing about the piece?

RL A bit. For some reason I'm thinking about adding in some vocal stuff, but want to talk to you about it first.

TK Now?

RL Tomorrow.

TK Is this a first, overlapping private and public dialogues, working on the work as it goes? I can't recall the dialogue in process and the work in process going public before.

RL How about in *Freeflow Returned* last September?

TK Not so live. The dialogues were more performative within the space. You couldn't step back and reflect like this.

RL It's not so reflective right now. The bus has filled and there are twenty of us heading off into the darkening rain. Polish, Russian, German, French and English is spoken on all sides. Hank and Sarah, from Canada, are planning their piece behind me 'the orange plastic ... so glad we brought the cardboard... did you pack a sewing kit? ... I was wondering if that might be ... ' and back to an ambient background of international murmur. This begins to feel like a journey without end, windows steaming up, chassis shuddering, engine noise, a lost little city bus with brittle seats. Music drifts from the driver's cab 'all by myself ... all by my ... self', like I am, this is it, the event, the festival and the place are a figment and a foible. I'm not really here, I'm out there talking to you. Then Jan, now sitting next to me, says 'We are here ... at least'.

7 APRIL 05
UPPER EAST SIDE, NEW YORK, USA

RL Bit of a strange night and morning.

TK Dreams?

RL I sat up late watching a DVD recording of Paul's one-hour TV interview on PBS. It went out in February.

TK He sounds like a high achiever.

RL The pundit said 'your curiosity knows no bounds' and kept referring to his knighthood and Nobel Prize.

TK An entertaining hour's viewing? I watched Desperate Housewives last night.

RL I don't know how to describe it. This dream interviewee was my boyhood friend from Perivale. I could imagine him becoming a national figure, the Stravinsky of science, New York's favourite emigré. So I woke with a renewed sense of urgency and ready to crack the day, the project and another *International Cleaning*.

TK Ready to achieve. Now let's not get into comparative values. Your urban interventions refresh my particular palate. Who watches PBS anyway? So how are we approaching this today?

RL Any ideas?

TK Always. Give me a minute ... we could focus on issues rather than events.

RL You mean ...

TK I mean let's cut to the essence of today and knock it around a bit.

RL *International Cleaning*?

TK Sure, but it doesn't need to be chronological.

RL This one was camera led. I thought about the shot for a couple of days, Queens Bridge in the background, best location Yorke Avenue and 81st Street. Video came first, as in Bangkok.

TK What's wrong with that?

RL Ask Ivan.

TK It's always gone hand in hand. Ignore him. He's never satisfied. This is an improving work, Richard, now in its fifth year. How will these video clips fit into our installation? I'd like some input.

RL Whatever you think.

TK Ivan appears in all of them, right? How many are there now?

RL Three in Bangkok, two in Prague, Brisbane, Perth, Los Angeles, Barcelona, Madrid, Frankfurt, three in Skyros, Singapore, Venice, Lillehammer, New York, Brooklyn, Providence, that's 20. Poland to come.

TK So how we show them is crucial. They have to be visually engaging or within an interesting framework or I don't want them in.

RL Is this because they pre-date our dialogues?

TK Hang on there, they've actually been a part of recent dialogues. Even in Skyros in August we returned to the Brooke statue because of a cleaning there the year before. I think you'd lost interest in the project till I came into the frame. The dialogues have re-invigorated them. And they had a place in *The Room of Freeflow* so far as I recall.

RL Would you like some input into, say, a London series?

TK Maybe. But I'm more concerned about how they'll be shown.

RL Any ideas?

TK In a clean space, minimal. Projected onto the floor or a series of objects. In a domestic setting. As a compilation interspersed with blanks and silence. As a centrepiece.

RL Really? I wasn't expecting you'd want them in.

TK We'll keep talking about it.

RL OK.

TK You won't get me cleaning. So, other issues of the day?

RL Art and shopping.

TK Financial constraints?

RL I was in a department store that Joshua recommended.

TK What's the issue here?

RL It wasn't until I overheard a shop assistant talking about how he was on the early shift 'the morning of 9/11' that I realised the store was right next to Ground Zero. I'd come in from a side entrance.

TK Century 21?

RL Yep. I felt pretty gloomy. It eased when you chose an unlikely shirt.

TK We chose it you mean.

RL Intuitively. Later I had lunch in a nearby sushi place and filmed the people passing the window. This mix of age, size, background and ethnicity would be a sample of those killed. I wept a little.

TK Is the issue to do with your emotions or intuition?

RL We haven't talked much about emotions previously.

TK Have you been scared to?

RL I don't know, I guess I've avoided it.

TK Art and feelings.

RL You don't express emotions in your art.

TK Don't talk rubbish.

RL Not obviously.

TK Of course. I bet you didn't film yourself weeping in the sushi bar.

RL Only a bit.

TK Jesus. And will you use that sequence?

RL Unlikely.

TK Why?

RL I'm not sure it was convincing, might look contrived.

TK That's my point. No need to overstate. Emotional content is bound up with the autobiographical for me. It's out there like a press story. Or it's subliminal. I think your position is more confused. You allude to emotion, you exploit it, you think it's substance just by revealing it.

RL Performance has occupied an emotional form for me, but not recently.

TK What about *Eleanor's Falcon*?

RL I abandoned that piece.

TK And performed it last year. Was the emotional content an issue? You spilt some beans there.

RL Probably.

TK So it's useful to talk about this.

RL ...

TK Reluctant agreement then. Like getting blood out of a stone. Let's go back to the sushi bar.

RL Or the other issue of the day.

TK Too close for comfort?

RL For now.

TK That's what I'm here for. Not letting you off the hook, out of the pan.

RL I think this one's more straightforward and more complex.

TK I'm intrigued.

RL It's relevant for us both.

TK Am I guessing?

RL No, I'm trying to find a way to express it.

TK My coffee's getting cold.

RL I think you'll like this one.

TK Go on.

RL It's about art, museums and galleries.

TK Big topic.

RL I'll narrow it down. To be honest, I didn't respond to the new wing of MoMA and I'm not sure you would have.

TK An off day?

RL It was about consumption and representation. I felt this wasn't my world. I know we're aiming *The Manifestation* at galleries but this experience left me cold. And there was something sad about the sculpture garden, with its fairly desultory collection arranged amongst self-conscious seating. The yellow Caro was flaking rust. The colossal security guard's posture was as interesting as the objects.

TK What are you driving at?

RL I'm not sure. I just wanted to share it with you, get your response.

TK I don't know what I'm responding to yet. You went to a big art museum and it left you cold. So what? Are you disillusioned with art or something?

RL With a certain kind of packaging and consumption.

TK One that I aspire to?

RL Yes.

TK Now I get it. We'll have to agree to differ on this one, or the whole project's in jeopardy.

RL Really?

TK Look, Richard, I realise you started the day in the shadows, but this is fucking ridiculous. Choice comes into it, you know. *International Cleaning*, shopping, tears, sushi and high art. Indigestion. Bad planning. Flakey behaviour. Leave me out of this one, I've got a career in the making.

2 APRIL 05
PROVIDENCE, RHODE ISLAND, USA

RL What would you like to know?

TK What do you want to tell me?

RL Feel kind of embarrassed.

TK Rubbish. Some sort of betrayal?

RL No.

TK What then?

RL The complexity of it.

TK Is that what you told them?

RL Yes.

TK That's a relief.

RL Why?

TK No reason to undersell, trivialise, encourage voyeurism.

RL It was the closest I've got to explaining our developing relationship. And you influenced this.

TK I would hope. How in particular?

RL Putting your early work in context. Explaining your background.

TK Ever thought about reinventing it?

RL Not till now.

TK What else?

RL The sense of a work in progress right there and then, including those materials sourced locally the day before: the large red envelopes, gold seals, snow scraper. Holding back decisions about where and how to place them, so you could be influential in keeping them tight on the table. Wearing the goat tie you chose in Bangkok. Picking up *In Praise of Shadows* at the last minute from Room 326 at The

Biltmore. Opening it at random on 'How, in such a dark place, gold draws so much light to itself is a mystery'.

TK What about our 'developing relationship'?

RL It's complicated. You change. I change. We've changed.

TK Too right, I don't hang around. How about the audience?

RL Meiling Cheng's paper on Claudia Bucher's Kinocognophores was fifteen pages long and took 45 minutes to read aloud. So I was held to 30 minutes max.

TK I can smell the tension.

RL You said it. Was oh so familiar, and being in competition with seventeen other concurrently programmed events was bizarre and undermining.

TK Really?

RL Just bizarre, I'm exaggerating. It was what it was. That's where you were so helpful.

TK In trying to keep you in the here and now, and treating it as a tester for so many situations to come, not getting into comparisons ...

RL Yes.

TK It was an opportunity. You wouldn't have progressed it this far without the pressure of the occasion, the output, the deadline.

RL Yes.

TK I'm remembering that you've given presentations about *The Room of Freeflow* a few times. Was this different?

RL The focus was much more on you and I, even declaring that we'd be talking for the rest of the day, and in New York for four days.

TK If you seriously demonstrate our relationship then you're representing me, and I expect a good profile. Did I get it?

RL I think so.

TK How did you deal with being classified under 'Altered Egos' in the programme? You got upset about this.

RL Didn't you?

TK I found it funny. So what did you do?

RL I expressed deep rage and forgiveness.

TK I think you're making progress.

RL Thanks.

TK How was the transition into the day, the stepping out?

RL Difficult, self-conscious, funny. I went along to a range of panel discussions and presentations pretty much on a whim, then bought a white designer fly swat at the Rhode Island School of Design store.

TK What sort of panel discussions?

RL The role of silence in Gertrude Stein's libretto for Virgil Thomson's The Mother of Us All, 'Arabesk' Kurdish underground music, the symbolised matrix of tying a stick to your leg so you limp, Kid Rock, Zhen Brasil's Japanese Brazilian Groove, Sha Xin Wei from the Georgia Institute of Technology talking about spatial syntax, embedded thresholds and the topology of gesture, etc.

TK Are we becoming self-conscious about these dialogues?

RL How do you mean?

TK Because we know they go public I think there's stuff we say purposely and stuff we don't reveal.

RL What should we do about it?

TK Acknowledge it for a start. See what needs to change. Talk.

RL I worry it's becoming formulaic.

TK You worry full stop. So what do you want to do differently?

RL Be more direct. Not feel pressurised to make things happen.

TK Did you?

RL I guess. Did some *Impotence* at the conference. Took some ground level photographs.

TK This wasn't my idea.

RL Shall we talk about it?

TK Let's get real.

RL I don't know what the relationship is between our dialogues and our allocated days here, I've lost track.

TK There never was a track. It's a blank page every time. Have you been looking for my approval or something? Are you leaping ahead to a secure position, like in windsurfing training phase one, holding on tight in case you fall in?

RL It's the pressure to be performative I think.

TK Performativity.

RL You taking the piss?

TK Word of the week apparently.

RL Too right. *PSi* fever. But it's also to do with what worked in Skyros.

TK That was then. What about *Freeflow Returned*?

RL Yes. That was more visual than performative.

TK We moved closer to exploring perception and minimal interventions in Thailand.

RL Can the dialogue become the work?

TK It has been all along. Trust me. Every context is different. And every time slot. In New York don't focus so much on audience. See what happens. Hang in the present tense.

24 MARCH 05
WEST BROMWICH, WEST MIDLANDS

TK Why Wednesbury Art Gallery, sounds like a day of the week?

RL It was recommended by Trevor from The Public. It's in a place called Wednesbury. We had a look at the building last month.

TK But why?

RL It has unique qualities. A purpose-built art gallery to house the now depleted collection of Mr Edwin Richards, a highly successful coach axle manufacturer with a penchant for art collecting. Designed by West Bromwich architects Wood & Kendrick, it's made of pressed red brick and terracotta, including four heads on the façade of Wren, Newton, Reynolds and Flaxman. At the opening in 1891 'many houses of the town were decorated with flags and bannerettes', clearly a big event. Convinced?

TK I'd have to see it. Remind me why you're there and what we're talking about.

RL It's another of the monthly *Exchange* events for The Public in and around West Bromwich. Meeting as artform, you remember.

TK The public meeting goes private, invitation required.

RL That's the plan. It reminds me of seeking out new venues for AIT's monthly communications meetings.

TK Is that the only parallel?

RL The events themselves are quite like the one-hour 'tea breaks' I organised that were more about bringing a diverse group of people together than having an agenda.

TK Did you do some of the inviting?

RL Yes.

TK Part of the work?

RL I'm not sure.

TK Did you do the inviting at AIT?

RL No.

TK Why?

RL It wasn't so practical, needed someone central to coordinate.

TK A woman by any chance?

RL I thought you were a post-feminist.

TK Keep thinking. Who turned up?

RL Birmingham artist Simon Walker, neighbourhood warden Tony Voegun, Vera Barnes chair of the Golden Oldies Club, Tony Carroll of the Black Country Chambers, regeneration officer Kathy James, Steve Langley from the Media Centre, student teacher Debbie Jopling, Pam and Roy Jackson from the Swann Village Action Group, Tom Wright of Lugg Industries, Orit and Jackie from The Public.

TK Mm, cheerful melange. So how did it go?

RL Anything in particular?

TK The food.

RL Ready-made round plastic platters from a large supermarket. Modest and varied.

TK Sounds hideous. Sufficient?

RL Yes.

TK As art?

RL The food?

TK No, the event.

RL I explained the thinking behind it at the beginning this time, the relationship to The Public, that it was my thing, not some kind of PR or research project about the slow-moving building, that this was an art event not a meeting.

TK Does calling it art make it art?

RL Help, man overboard.

TK Well?

RL You know I'm deliberately exploring borderline territory. It's art and not art.

TK It's important to me to see it as art.

RL Why?

TK To keep your feet on the ground. Stop you drifting off into a la-la land of vague social worthiness that's hard to comprehend.

RL But don't you think it's difficult for people to accept this work as just art?

TK No I don't. You invite them. You set the tone. You make the thing happen. Of course it overlaps with daily life events, but it's your job to demarcate not obfuscate. This seems crucial or they won't know what they've been to or why.

RL Supposing they don't get it.

TK That's not your problem. Spelling it out in your terms is enough, and part of the intrinsic aesthetic.

RL And the group photo?

TK Likewise. And anything else you decide to introduce. They come from the root of the work, not from responding to need.

RL There has to be a bit of that.

TK Why?

RL For example, if no-one gets the point of receiving the group photo through the post.

TK If you really feel the need to follow-up why not do what Orit suggests and ask them what they made of it at a later date. But I wouldn't bother. Just invite them all back to the concluding one in July. I sometimes think you've gone too much over to the other side. Was there an aesthetic high point today, by the way?

RL I led a tour of the building. In the main gallery there was a centrepiece of chairs, arranged in opposite directions like a zipper. I asked people to fill these chairs, saying this was probably a first fill, then for a volunteer to play the grand piano. And there was one.

TK What?

RL A volunteer.

TK Who?

RL It was Debbie Jopling as it happens. Who were you thinking?

TK I imagined Pam and Roy tinkling some keys, side by side.

RL As Debbie played we sat there like it was meant to be.

TK Was it their highlight too?

RL Who?

TK The others.

RL I don't care, really.

TK Finally.

12 FEBRUARY 05
KOH SAMED, THAILAND

TK I'm not feeling very responsive. You've been talking about the dialogue or meeting as 'the work' and meanwhile neglecting this dialogue with me as 'work'.

RL Not intentionally.

TK Maybe. How about if these stories unfold through the dialogue. I imagine you have a list in mind, but there's also a lot of background to cover, geography alone.

RL But last time we spoke you proposed isolating key moments and leaving out the background.

TK I know. That was then. Leave it to me. So what's Koh Samed like?

RL A small island, quite developed, busier at the weekends, people visit from Bangkok. It's a designated nature reserve, without walking trails. I'm staying at Ao Prao, quite secluded, fairly exclusive.

TK And you're working? Facilitating, like you do on Skyros?

RL Yes.

TK Are you being reticent?

RL It's Saturday, my day off.

TK Is that the only reason?

RL It's not been an easy transition, from relative freedom to position of responsibility. In Greece last July it was the other way round. Our dialogues happened after the 'job' had ended. I was let loose and felt freer to engage with you.

TK So that's why you've been incommunicado. Talk to me.

RL Oh ...

TK I guess I have to see your resistance as a process ... it can be retrospective.

RL In the Bangkok Sofitel Hotel lobby, at the point of departure, of switching roles, responsibility looming, I left the video camera on a table and moved in and out of shot, around elaborate flower arrangements and attentive staff, unnoticed, almost. It was poignant, a desperate parting shot.

TK Or a declaration of intent. Not transition but fuck-off focus. From here on it all looks different. The flowers were for you, not the punters. The lobby designed for this exact moment, your passing through. The physical and cultural space shifting. Know what I mean?

RL It's taken a while to get back there, five days on this island, with occasional glimpses.

TK Like?

RL Like the heavy German on the beach waving his arms dismissively as I walked around his tripod. He was still there after the swim and I noticed this was no video camera but Super 8, a classic black machine. He told me enthusiastically that 'Kodak now guarantee their film for 100 years. Long enough, long enough ...'

TK What kind of glimpse was this?

RL Of an authentic relationship to the moving image; tech talk in tourist land.

TK How about in your teaching, the sensory awareness stuff?

RL It may sound naff.

TK Good. Try me.

RL I guess *The Silent Walk* was originally designed for artists, although the roots of it came from this work. And it's always memorable in some way.

TK Give me two details.

RL I arranged a line of chairs in the shrinking shade, facing out to sea and trees. We sat alongside each other watching and listening to the leaves falling. So unlike a European autumn: large heavy leaves taking their time, landing crisply on the wooden decking, a random act of nature.

TK And?

RL Towards the end of the walk we sat on a distant beach, hanging out, silently communicating or not, exploring, sitting, whatever. I'd experienced before the unspoken negotiation that happens between people on the walk, but this time I had a sense of the potential aesthetic subtlety of all relationships.

TK I don't get this. I'm not sure I want to.

RL It was through the silence. We weren't clowning around or miming. It was a quiet communication and awareness that seemed near perfect. We spend so much time struggling with speech that these qualities are maybe drowned out. That was how it looked. Does it make sense?

TK I'm taking it in, silently.

RL You taking the piss?

TK Let's stop talking for a while.

* * *

RL Ban Phe.

TK What?

RL That's where I've just been. Off and out, the mainland, with cameras.

TK You sound desperate.

RL After Bangkok the island is a tourist world that I've been struggling to find a relationship with. It's coming.

TK I don't believe you.

RL OK. It's driving me nuts. It's vacuous and Western. I miss Bangkok.

TK Isn't this also about psychological space? And don't I come into it? I mean we haven't spoken for days and things were happening in Bangkok, for sure.

RL Yes. Ban Phe was about taking off to the mainland and talking to you again, even though we didn't speak directly. It was about reclaiming my identity as an artist or 'flaneur' or social freak.

TK A cloud of surprised sanity breaks out. I need more.

RL I walk off in the intense heat along the main street towards the market and beyond. We've been told that Ban Phe consists of one main street. But there's more, and soon I'm a lone foreigner. Hundreds of small white squids are drying in grids on racks. I start to take photographs, or digital images.

TK Meaningful, focussed or documentary?

RL I'm not sure. More important that I'm actually in the process of taking them after a five day gap.

TK Any video?

RL No.

TK Anything performative?

RL No.

TK Perceptual?

RL That's what I'm coming to.

TK I thought the squids were it.

RL Sorry, just setting the scene. There's a parallel road behind the main waterside street, so I take this and come across a Buddhist complex. Lots of temples in here, and a monastery, very relaxed atmosphere. Gamelan music is playing quite loudly. A group of people are sitting on metal chairs listening to it, I assume. So I join them. A woman brings me cola in a plastic cup and I sit and sip, like it's the blood of Christ, taking it all in. No-one bothers me. I reach for the video camera but can't do it.

TK Why not?

RL It feels too intrusive. Jerome talked about this in Bangkok. As a photo-journalist on assignment in East Timor or Banda Aceh there were times when he couldn't take photos. He'd be letting his employers down for the sake of his psyche.

TK Are we there then? Is this the moment?

RL Yes, I'm in a kind of creative paralysis, and a total sensory absorption.

3 FEBRUARY 05
BANGKOK, THAILAND

TK I've changed my mind.

RL What about?

TK Giving my view of Tuesday.

RL Fine.

TK Well? I'm ready.

RL Right. What was your view of Tuesday, Tania?

TK It was Jerome's day. You were negotiating your relationship with him and the city. This may explain what was going on with you in Barcelona. Twelve years is a long time. I like him. He's fallible. It's a relationship, like you and me. You worked together, we're working together. Monday was also about relationships. It's going to plan.

By the way, did you get up to much, it wasn't clear?

RL A little *Impotence* at the theatre complex, with Jerome on camera.

TK Were you more production focused then?

RL I spent the morning talking to Varsha and figuring out when to move to the new accommodation.

TK What new accommodation?

RL She had relatives arriving from Hong Kong and Singapore, but there was her friend's empty apartment not too far away, just by the golf driving range off Soy 26.

TK Don't try and impress me with your new found familiarity with Bangkok street names.

RL We scheduled the move for 4pm. I met up with Jerome at 2pm back in the hotel coffee shop. He didn't buy anything. We occupy different economies. He lives here and doesn't take the Sky Train. There are eight cheaper forms of transport. We had just under two hours for *International Cleaning*.

TK This feels familiar. You're cramming it in, stuffing the shopping in the basket. You don't know what you're buying.

RL I thought it would be ample time, but we were rushed. I also wanted the chance to talk before he flew. It could be another twelve years.

TK Unlikely. Why did *International Cleaning* take priority?

RL Not sure, seemed like the right approach, and I'd planned to stage at least one here in Bangkok, ticking off another global destination.

TK Couldn't the conversation have taken priority.

RL It was too tempting to recreate past experience, with him on camera, me doing things.

TK A kind of conversation after all.

RL And a collaboration. What a relief to have someone trusted on camera, who also knew the city and the people.

TK Did you have locations in mind?

RL No, but we didn't need to look far. I think we made three altogether, and another *Impotence* beside the massively busy road Sukhumvit.
I cleaned –
1 A Honda-equivalent Harley Davidson
2 Some vegetation
3 A lamppost with a vast gold backdrop ad for 'The Best King Ever' in English.
– all with a cloth borrowed from Varsha.
The motorbike was parked on the pavement. Jerome went into the shop and asked permission on my

behalf, said I was going round the world cleaning things. They said OK.

TK They would. Have you looked over any of the video yet?

RL Not yet.

TK What was it like saying goodbye?

RL OK. Sad. We'll exchange emails while he's in China. I introduced him to Varsha and it looks like he'll be included in a photography show she's curating here in March. It feels ongoing. What's your view?

TK Nice networking. Shame it wasn't for my benefit. Right now I'm more interested in how you worked together than in the footage he shot of you 'doing' things. I can imagine it without seeing it. I'd prefer you to experience these days as a continuum of experience, along with the other stuff that you don't tell me about.

RL What other stuff?

TK Like shopping or taxi rides, or more of your reactions to the sex industry, your fears and excitements. It can all be different levels of the same attuned perceptual state. Why don't you give it a go right now.

RL I feel scared and overwhelmed just thinking about it. Have I been using Jerome as a screen? The interventions are making my imprint, forming my relationship with the amoral smiling wonderful chaos. I'm fearless of traffic, in position at the side of the road, straight suit. There's an elephant on the street, a chicken in a brick in the market for a pound, a teenager for sale in every other bar for the fat guy from Margate who knows where to go. Ain't no tourist. Don't make me hold your hand and pay your way back to Burma with dick cash. I'm a visiting artist amongst others: Varsha Nair, Jerome Ming, Lee Wen, Chumpon Apisuk. I'm here to talk to you Tania. Public money paid for the fucking airline ticket. I'm forgetting.

23 OCTOBER 04 · BARCELONA, SPAIN

RL It's not working. This is no good. It's all going wrong. I'm walking around the fish market pointing the camera at my face. I put this time aside. As if that was enough. And remembering that bit from the penultimate day in Greece.

TK Which?

RL In the Plateia at night, I walk and read aloud from Sophocles, video camera at arm's length.

TK That was a long time coming. You can't expect it to have the same impact in another context altogether.

RL I did.

TK I thought you'd learnt this one by now. You were rushing.

RL I was rushing. I was out of it.

TK Out of step.

RL Literally. Desperate. Awful. Disempowered.

TK You kept it to yourself.

RL Mournful. Sightless. Overtaken by sensation of people, fish and marble slabs.

TK Too much preconception. Not enough awareness. Anything?

RL Nothing.

TK Cut the angst. Time off. Time out. Get a coffee.

RL Something else.

TK Get some froth on it. Lighten up.

RL It is.

TK What?

RL Lighter.

TK Like a lighter.

RL My finger.

TK Not in the terrain of the chorizo. Keep your hands in your pockets.

22 OCTOBER 04
BARCELONA, SPAIN

TK Holà.

RL This is a different kind of situation.

TK Here you go again. It always is.

RL Things have moved on since Berlin.

TK Why are you on about Berlin again?

RL Maybe because Jens is here. It's an exquisite dilemma, doing or not doing.

TK These conversations can be the thing. No doubt you've been at it though.

RL Doing?

TK Yes ... go on then.

RL What?

TK Open the box.

RL I'm not sure where it came from.

TK What?

RL *Standing Very Still.*

TK It came from Skyros. We talked about it, 'standing still where the animals are', and at the Dioni Hotel.

RL You're right. So that's where it came from. But this time it was about movement and stillness. It was the platform of the Barcelona Metro. I stand motionless at the edge. The train comes in. The doors open and close. It moves off. I remain fixed.

TK Sounds like a video work to me.

RL A bit like *International Cleaning*, this one could run and run, but had to see it back on video, yes.

TK OK. Enough. I get the picture. It needs a new name.

RL Any ideas?

TK Fixation, Static, Impotence.

RL Static?

TK Impotence.

RL If you insist.

TK I do. It's better.

RL Alright then. That wasn't all. *Impotence* was repeated at the Parc Guell. By me, then Jens standing in for me. He was on camera, I was on camera. Back in tourist land. Then some footage of shoes amongst columns.

TK Whose shoes?

RL Mine and other peoples, mine looked weird. Then the shoe saga.

TK Now you're talking.

RL It was obsessive, looking for two pairs of Camper shoes in their homeland, shop to shop, all over the city. It became a mission of forlorn hopelessness, a consumerist folly.

TK Why didn't you ask me?

RL I didn't think of it.

TK Are these shoes to perform in?

RL Probably.

TK Did this start to feel like *The Day of the Moped*?

RL Yes.

TK So what can you take from this?

RL 'What shoes are' maybe?

TK And clothes in general. Were you taken as a tourist, wearing the suit?

RL No.

TK That's what I mean. You brought the suit with you deliberately. We discussed this. So, buying Camper shoes in Spain, shoes that you work in, is not just about footwear. I'm sure you'd planned this purchase beforehand.

RL Mm.

TK Is it more function than fashion, more identity than image?

RL It's all mixed up, interconnected.

TK The shoe as icon, like the suit.

RL I guess so. I feel a bit embarrassed to be admitting this.

TK It's all there, very clear, you've just been trying to ignore it. You're being coy.

RL How come we have so much to say about this?

TK Because it's dominated your afternoon. Because it went wrong. And these are interesting situations – in a strange city, trying to find a pair of shoes that are elusive, that maybe don't exist, that perhaps aren't right anyway. The absurdity of it. That you left me out of it. That you once worked in a shoe factory. That you'd filmed your feet that morning and your shoes looked wrong, and these were the same shoes you wore in Greece: what does that say about Barcelona? You were tortured by guilt at the thought of buying two pairs of shoes and likewise guilt-ridden about not having talked to me for hours, only Jens. And you're Piscean, both of you. It's all quite funny.

RL Do you mean it serves me right?

TK I mean it's OK with me if you have a hard time. Why shouldn't you? I mean that every situation is unique. It's like I said in Greece – it doesn't matter what you do, it's the awareness that counts. And you lost it.

RL It had occurred to me that the piece of action at the Metro could have been enough for the whole day.

TK Sure. But why try and exclude me? A bit of tokenistic filming of mosaics at Sagrada Familia or the Parc Guell doesn't do it for me. You know that.

RL Fair enough. Sorry. What shoes are you wearing, by the way?

TK Red leather designer trainers. As if.

19 SEPTEMBER 04
CHISENHALE, BETHNAL GREEN, LONDON

RL I could do with a break.

TK Sorry.

RL Really?

TK I'd like to be there, Richard, and not just to give you a break ...

RL I'm not convinced. Anyway, your works have been getting attention.

TK Surprised?

RL A bit. I thought this installation was the thing, *Freeflow Returned*. Maybe your pieces are easier on the eye, and the brain.

TK I do know what I'm doing, as a matter of fact. I want my work to communicate more clearly than yours. And it does. It sells, you know.

RL Two guys came in a while ago, may have been a gay couple.

TK What's their orientation got to do with it?

RL Nothing, only they looked like they were home-making, checking out your work to see if it fitted their décor. I was worried because I thought they were going to ask the price of one of your wall pieces.

TK I thought we'd talked about pricing?

RL Not really.

TK I left a price list.

RL I didn't see it.

TK Jesus, Richard.

RL Well, you should have been here. Anyway, they didn't ask in the end.

TK I don't think you really wanted to show my work, at all.

RL Yes, I did.

TK And it was all from 2002. I've moved on so much since then. You could have dated it, you dated most of the other stuff. And you know I wasn't comfortable with you showing this body of work.

RL You can't have everything.

TK Maybe I can. This is my career we're talking about.

RL But the overall installation was the main thing for me, I thought it was for you.

TK It's not as simple as that. It was essentially your studio, remember, that I'd been sub-letting, your stuff was everywhere, I had to claim some space. And this was an 'open studio' event, the kind of thing I rarely agree to.

RL OK, but you know you had a major influence on how it looked.

TK And how it was conceived.

RL Yes.

TK Why do I get the feeling that you're giving me credit and not giving me credit at the same time?

RL For Christ's sake, Tania, you've been credited as a collaborator on the door as people come in, your name is up beside your wall and floor pieces, what else was I supposed to do?

TK It's more to do with your thinking than your actions.

RL Collaboration is never easy for me. I think it's gone well.

TK Limp excuses. You think you're easy to work with? Did you ever ask me?

RL I'm sure I did. Well let me ask you now.

TK Fine. Go ahead.

RL How do you think the collaboration went, Tania?

TK It's been revealing. I liked the concept of the overlap between studio and artwork, so process became practice. But that was more about a relationship with your studio practice rather than mine.

RL Anything else?

TK Give me a chance. I enjoyed participating, drawing your attention to things, like encouraging you to go for the tepee construction and *Get Shirty in Process*. But it could have gone the other way round too. My work was never the chosen starting point, so you had to show some of my pieces to balance things out.

RL I'm feeling criticised here.

TK That's your problem, not mine. Am I right, though?

RL You only seem to see things from your perspective.

TK And you? I hear a lot about your perspective. I thought you'd asked for mine.

RL OK. But we are at different stages in our careers.

TK So what. We're talking about a real experience here, a semi-public showing, with both our names credited. I'd like some recognition that goes beyond your titles on the wall and credits on the door.

RL From me?

TK Yes.

RL Right ... I'd like to work with you again, Tania. Does that seem like recognition?

TK On an installation?

RL Yes, but maybe on other stuff too.

TK With a proper public profile?

RL Yes. Are you interested?

TK Sure. I think we've just scratched the surface, turned the corner, crossed the line, started the real talk. This was never going to be the end of it.

18 SEPTEMBER 04
BETHNAL GREEN, LONDON

TK Is this too close for comfort?

RL How do you mean? You really asking this?

TK We're in your studio space for real, both of us, not like *The Room of Freeflow*, which was a neutral space. Or in Australia, with an installation to represent the three studios, your two and my one. Here we're actually in one of them, or two of them. My early pieces have been stored in here in boxes, for real.

Like, is there a reason why there hasn't been an *International Cleaning* in London?

RL You mean too close to home?

TK Yes.

RL I think the stakes are higher. This is where it all began, the ideas for Firstsite, an awareness of studio-as-process, tools as archaeology, etc. It's easier sitting in a beach bar in Skyros discussing ideas, there's less at stake, less revealed maybe. It's no coincidence that we're talking differently, less anecdotally.

To be honest with you, I've started to see this as a possible format for a gallery show, a framework that could hold many smaller elements, like *International Cleaning*, where process and studio hold it all together.

TK Respect please. I already had that idea. So what happens at the end of this?

RL Good question. One to ponder. Private and public. Exposed and revealed.

TK I'd like to go through my contribution to all this.

RL OK.

TK *The Takeaway Table. The Tepee.* The use of materials and the line between studio and work. The social side – how people have reacted.

RL For me it's been about titles, especially *Kite Fragments, Fireside Chair* and *Red Box.*

TK My choices of music. Taking on the *Window Piece* here and now, rather than putting it off.

RL Abandoned and forgotten pieces, including *Handles for Didcot.*

TK Treading that line. I sound like you now.

RL Which line?

TK In and out of behind the scenes, in the public eye, the visitor crossing the threshold, in the work, at the typewriter, London 04, Toronto 84, two studios, two windows, views almost the same, now, not then, your grandfather's chair that your father sat on that's become the focal point of the tepee structure, the varnished oak frame, the cans of paint strewn around, the work in progress. Are you working or performing? Am I there or not? Are you feeling tired because you're trying to think what to write as you sit and type, or because you're on display, another element in the work, a quirky host?

RL I'm exhausted, drained. It doesn't let up till I walk out at the end of the day. It starts as soon as the door opens.

TK The maker welcomes you. Come in to my home. Come in. Look at me. Look at her work. Don't look at me. Talk to me. Don't talk to me. Talk to her. You occupy the space. But don't be surprised who comes through the door. Your door. Your privacy doesn't exist, don't kid yourself. My absence is colossal.

8 AUGUST 04
SKYROS, GREECE

TK What do you want to talk about?

RL Sunday and its significance for us.

TK Anything about the day off?

RL It was 24 hours, starting 11am Saturday.

TK But I can't imagine a complete detachment. You've been talking about a continuum.

RL It was a relief not to be working. Although in the afternoon we're back at the Hotel Dioni pool and this time I'm covered in temporary tattoos: work and leisure intertwined again.

On Sunday morning ideas begin to surface. I swim ashore and collect bamboo roots and stems from the beach, placing them beside the moped.

TK So, we're talking retrospectively again, it's Monday morning now.

RL Yes. I'm sitting in the Plateia, not sure of the time, probably about 9.45am. Yannis is sporting a short white jacket this morning, the kind that dentists wear. I'm listening to a pirate CD from one of the Nigerian street-sellers. Their clunky backpacks are laden with illicit music. This one works. Lounge music. *Café del Mar*. *Volumen Diez*. Mixed by Bruno.

TK Bruno Moldari?

RL It doesn't say.

TK He's a friend of my brother. It's probably him.

RL On the moped I took a different route, stopping off at the new supermarket to look for string, and bought two fly swats.

TK My idea?

RL Kind of. This was definitely our most collaborative day.

TK Pleased to hear it.

RL For some reason I'd also been recalling a temporary installation in Poland in '97, with washing lines stretched between two vehicles. It took an age to set up but didn't quite work.

TK Surely we've gone beyond the language of 'working' or not?

RL Maybe that's what made me think of it. Similar with *White on White*: an unrealised, unresolved idea.

TK I've noticed other notes on your studio wall about focusing on failed or abandoned concepts.

RL By the way, how's the sublet going?

TK It's a bit damp, but I like the space. Good timing for me, a lot on. How did we get on to this?

RL The search for string.

TK That led to fly swats.

RL Yes.

TK Present tense.

RL It's a different start to the day.

TK It's a different day.

RL It's the last day on the island and I'd like to explore some of the thoughts or ideas for the project, ones we haven't covered yet.

TK You sound like an artist.

RL Do I? Maybe I feel like one today.

TK What's the difference?

RL More visual. A different relation to the notebook. The deadline. Your input?

TK It's not just input, it's a process that's been building over the week. I'm integral you realise.

RL Of course. Plenty to refer to from previous days, lots to do, and not to do.

I park in the shade near the Ferugia beach bar and purposely enter wearing the silver crash helmet. I spread out across a table, take the long paintbrushes from the rucksack, then the fly swats, orange and red. I operate the video camera, then the phone. I'm exploring, mostly, what the camera sees and hears. It's a version of *The Table Project*. The orange fly swat against the silver helmet, then filming through it to dog and sea beyond. There's a performative element. Seamless. Inconsequential. Nothing and a little something.

I'm reminded of 12 months ago, working in the Park Caffeen and how I behaved in the quieter moments between serving customers, improvising with tables, looking around through the camera lens. But the 'work/art' issue has changed.

TK You're referencing a lot of artworks today.

RL Maybe I'm less self-conscious about the whole thing.

TK It's more than that. I think you're in an easier nether-world than two days ago, a more workable one. I'm enjoying the detail. Can you be objective and remember how you made decisions?

RL I'll try. I was thinking about how I'd like to reveal the presence of the camera to the camera. Then rule this out as I'd need another camera. As I leave the bar I sense the response of other people and play on this a little. Still looking for string, I stop at the supermarket on the beach road. No string but I hear you saying, 'Buy what you can'. I find small straw sweeping brushes, masking tape, clothes pegs, coloured plastic straws, moped décor.

TK No streamers, thank Christ.

RL I take the steep road up to Brooke Square and know exactly what I want to do. I relocate the camera position from two years ago and recall how invisible I was as a cleaner. Greek tourists are clustered in groups photographing themselves, as usual. I place the camera at a lower level, the complete statue in shot and press record. I take out Sophocles and start to walk in clockwise circles around the statue, reading aloud. I'm not invisible. I can't be. But they carry on with their photography. I'm csik. I've gone. My voice grows louder. I emphasise certain phrases, occasionally whispering, occasionally stopping at the camera, gesturing and repeating words. I take my shirt off and continue.

The square is now empty. Tourists occasionally come and go. This feels like a public space of huge resonance. Here is the muse of poetry with rippling bronze muscles, here a discreet relief of Rupert's face, and there's a sense of permission all around me. I'm an Englishman taking care of the square. I know about this statue that's not Rupert. He was no Adonis but a soft boy.

I feel utterly empowered. I play with the words over and over. They are becoming my own: 'Pitiful, you suffer so, you understand so much – I wish you had never known' – 'You've suffered so much, it's pitiful. You understand so much of this – if only you'd never known' – 'The pity of it, your suffering, your understanding – who told you?' – 'Pity you, pity us all, the pity of it –' I reclaim these resonances of desperation sanitised into English by Robert Fagles, taking them away from a certain kind of theatre.

Am I Rupert on his deathbed out there at sea, a volcanic rock, or that fly facing its own mortality?

I start to pack up. Then you intervene.

TK Not before time.

RL It's something like, lose your head, Richard.

TK It was more like, don't hold back.

RL Whatever. I take out the red fly swat and enthusiastically whack the calves of the statue. There is a fly, in fact, but I aim to miss him. The sound of plastic on bronze is to relish. I clamber up the pedestal and keep on going, fragments of red plastic breaking off as I give him a good spanking.

TK I've got someone coming round in ten minutes, can you précis the rest?

RL Oh. Well, what do you think so far?

TK A little danger in the territory always makes me smile. It's been a collaborative day. No judgements from me. I want to see the video. We need to put some time aside to reflect on the whole thing. There's more to come. We're going global.

4 AUGUST 04
SKYROS, GREECE

TK Another day starts. I imagine you taking the 8am bus, finding a café and writing in your High Notes No2 book before heading for the internet café.

RL I sat in Yannis' in the Plateia. He's easy company in the early morning. Quiet activity around the square. Darren and Sharon joined me at the two other terminals in the internet café while I sent off some text to Andrew in London.

TK Convenient coupling?

RL She's thinking of changing her name.

TK Smart move.

RL They were driving back across the island to Atsitsa, so I could pick up Simon's moped, which I'd arranged to use while he's in Turkey.

TK I don't need to know about Simon. But you having a moped changes things.

RL I got quite excited and hit a bit of 'flow', as Csikszentmihalyi would call it; or in-touch-ness, as I'd call it.

TK For me, it's a groove, a kicking-in, a 'don't distract me or I'll lose it'. We claim it as artists but Csik would say we can all access it, I imagine. Let's formalise this state as 'csik' for in the groove and 'spill' for when you're out of it.

RL Good idea. It was quite a brief csik, the few minutes before we drove off, but long enough for two thoughts, ideas, intuitions, whatever we want to call them. I saw a couple of local people sitting on low walls near the supermarket, where the Lada was parked. I thought about the tradition of 'sitting' here and how sitting could be added to *Standing Very*

Still. I also thought about the moped as a sculptural icon: have already explored this in Utica, Upstate New York with *Rent-A-Car*, but this was more about being on the bike as performer, bike as collaborator, maybe decorated. What do you think?

TK Potential in both. I expect your first thought was to attach streamers to the back of it. But we can work on something less obvious, less decorative.

RL Like?

TK More to do with you and bike, you on bike, in transition, place to place, passing people who see you, person and object in motion. Anyway, what's it like?

RL It's an old Honda, 50cc I think. It was parked on a dirt road, covered in a polythene sheet. I picked up the helmet from under Colin's bed in Hut 38, said hello to Yannis and Mateja, bumped into Peter, Philippa and Ben in their hire car. They were looking for a picnic spot. Peter said I had a flat back tyre. He was right, but with the complications of finding someone who might be able to help and getting drawn into long conversations, I decided it was best to head off and sort it out in Skyros Town, at the petrol station on the way in.

TK You daredevil.

RL Really. The tyre got flatter by the minute. By the time I reached Yiurgo's taverna a mile up the road it had developed a distinctive limp. At every revolution the back wheel went over its own integral bump. I assumed this to be the inner tube valve.

TK I didn't realise you were an experienced moped rider.

RL I'm not. This was scary. I stopped at the taverna, hoping that Yiurgos, one of the island's most advanced bikers, would be around. He wasn't. The

Russian waitress looked at the wheel, shrugged and said 'one minute' then sat down again. Not convinced by this I decided to motor on, slowly and hopefully.

TK How far was it?

RL I'm not sure exactly. From there, maybe 12 miles.

TK Were you able to incorporate this erratic riding experience into the project? Did it become work?

RL I tried, but fear was taking over. The bike was very unstable, especially on corners and uneven surfaces. By now the inner tube had separated itself and was flapping around the tyre like a failed condom, so I stopped again and yanked out pieces of rubber. I know this road well, but travelling it at 10 mph was a new experience.

TK So by my calculations this was an hour or so well spent.

RL Must have been. There was the odd moment when I did experience this noisy, limping, rattling motion-in-time with my own physical bumping and lurching as an equivalent to *Standing Very Still*.

TK Nice effort. It's the relationship to fear that interests me. The 'fear in tandem with creative risk' thing.

RL You're right. If it hadn't been for our project this would have been just plain irritating and scary, especially as trucks passed me while I crawled and bounced over the desolate mountain pass. But I kept thinking of you, and how we could make this into something.

TK It reminds me of the previous evening at the Plateia festival, where the seemingly least relevant experience was the most challenging artistically.

RL That's true. But I had no choice here, as this gradually unfolded as *The Day of the Moped*. I decided to pass the petrol station and go straight to the moped shop in town, where Simon had bought this ex-rental machine for 250 Euros. Fortunately, I arrived just before siesta at 1·25pm. Unfortunately, I was told they don't fix these old bikes any longer and the only place to go was the petrol station I'd passed 15 minutes earlier.

It was now siesta time, the island's pride, the longest siesta in the western world. I felt the pressure of doing some 'work', some 'action', have some lunch and taking a siesta myself. Had the video camera survived the journey? The bike could be sorted out later. I'd arrived.

TK You were struggling with some dubious conscience. Could you see the funny side?

RL Not yet. I had a brief siesta at Ari's place and decided to spend an hour on the project, our project, this project, before returning to the wounded vehicle.

TK Interesting separation.

RL Yes, like at the hotel pool. Stepping out of his door and into the field below was entering art space. In theory. This was a chance to explore *Working With Animals*. A chicken and her chicks scuttered off in front of me, but that was it. No donkey, no mule, no horse. Gone.

TK I sense an insight is overdue.

RL I couldn't find it yet. Did some *Standing Very Still*, looking out into the landscape. And I did go into sensory space. It was a relief, no longer in staggering motion, stillness was ecstatic. I began to focus on temperature, then sound, hearing birds, dogs, insects, then... a moped. And I felt this terrible lurch of jealousy. A moped that works. Then another, and another. Emotions were taking over and I gradually came back out, returned to the video camera, noticing a barcode floating in space on a dumped cardboard box.

Walking back up the hill I glanced at two parked mopeds, with good back tyres. Now I was experiencing full-blown moped envy. I was on fire and could think of nothing else.

TK Seriously?

RL Yes. Even my one hour of 'work' had been interrupted by the moped issue, so I gave into it and went back to where it was parked. Approaching the Plateia from the back road I saw again a neglected multi-faceted wall that would be good to work with at some point.

The bike looked innocent and appealing – TMA 2131 – except for the back tyre. A bearded priest was approaching in traditional Greek Orthodox black robe and flat hat. I was now astride the machine and willed him, of all people, not to comment on the state of my wheel. He did. This shoved me into a slightly new zone. If he could comment then everyone must be aware of it. I would drive and wave, drive and nod, in full acknowledgement of my condition. I was going in.

TK I mentioned yesterday that I don't so much care what happens over these days. I see the focus as less to do with action, more on acceptance, perception and awareness, and the transitions between in and out, csik and spill, you and me.

RL But I do find it hard to trust that anything's going to happen.

TK Tell me about it. This is hard work. Are you really listening?

RL Yes, and trying.

TK So you're getting there.

RL The welcoming flags of the petrol station finally appeared. I'd been rehearsing my gestures of despair. I slapped hand on head, pointing to tyre. He looked reluctant. But he would fix it. Or try to. He manoeuvred it across so that the back wheel hovered over a concrete pit. He could access it from below. Then someone turned up for petrol and he was off, gone. And so it went. It took as long to get this fixed as my journey across the island. But this time I went with it as far as I could, with video camera and notebook.

Ilias arrived for petrol, the only English speaker of the island's eight taxi drivers. He translated for me 'He say in such a bad state he must change tyre as well. Who pay?' I'll pay. Thanks Ilias. Situation now clear, but slow. I began to will passing drivers not to stop for petrol, but 50% did. Not speaking Greek, I start to imagine what's being said between the performers in this theatre of motoring: 'This back tyre's a bit flat ... Someone went into me just there ... Where's Yannis? ... I got this new wheel, is it the same size as the busted one? Look at the size of that hole in the tyre, went right through ... What the hell are you doing? Can't you help me fix this bloody moped tyre. What a shit job ... Leave the wheel there, we'll sort it out for you, I can't do everything at once... I've got this tourist here waiting for his moped, keeps writing in his book... How's it going, man? ... OK, fill it up yourself ... '

I've now started to see aspects of the physical space as an installation, and become aware of its physical location before the backdrop of hills and the town on crater-top beyond. I now see the writing as an act of performance, and also work on developing a macho stance of impatience and resignation.

I've entered the arena. Now I work here. I stare at the motorists as they get out of their driver's seats, often awkwardly. 'Here, you finish the bloody thing while I sort the tractor out ... Can you put some oil in for me? ... Super Unleaded? ... Yep ... Did you fill it right up? ... Yep ... OK, bye ... Like the way she bounces, man, heh, heh, heh ... '

An eight year-old girl arrives quietly with her push-bike. 'You got a flat tyre, lovey? Oh dear, let's have a look for you.' If you'd been here, Tania, if you'd been riding this fucking thing, they'd have fixed it for you in no time. I write you a text message:

Wits end moped fiasco. You'd have been served an hour ago. Life as art is all about perception. Am I really an irate customer or in the groove? I can be tough. Rx

You reply:

Cool it RL. It's the Greek way. This is your day. What does it mean? It's OK with me. Get your perception going. Stop writing. Go for the in. Be satisfied. Tx

Finally, I drive off smoothly towards the sea as the sun sets over the volcanic plug behind me. I stand still on the beach in the fading light, looking out to the horizon, and make some very slow arm movements. I recall teaching Steven Berkoff Tai Chi three weeks ago a mile or so from here, and how he wanted to 'make it his own'. Light is fading, waves are lapping and this is mine, all mine.

6 JUNE 04
WEST BROMWICH, WEST MIDLANDS

TK So how do you think they went, Richard, the three 'public meetings' you held yesterday 'in the historic Council Chamber of West Bromwich Town Hall'?

RL OK, I think.

TK A little elaboration would be nice.

RL Well ... I had some last-minute thoughts on Friday evening after the Guillermo Gomez-Peña performance lecture and in the morning. I made a note of some of them:

- be prepared to be anarchic
- Dennis, dj and mixer, stays for all three meetings
- make a movie
- someone takes minutes
- keep notes
- inhabit the space
- all technical people become 'special guests'
- improvise

That kind of thing.

TK So?

RL So just about all of these late entries found their place, took pole position even.

TK Isn't that often the case when the pressure rises?

RL Always a surprise though. Anyway, what did you think of them?

TK More questions first.

RL This is like an interrogation.

TK Or an interview. Rest easy, I'm on a track here. So ... I suspect you'd given some thought to your persona as the chair and this was quite fundamental to the piece. But I thought a key issue for you was to look again at the work/art overlap, so your role moved close to the kind of person who normally chairs this kind of meeting. Right?

RL Yes. But it all shifted a bit with these late changes. They'd been advertised on posters and in local papers as regular public meetings open to anyone. That was the point. As the chair, I did picture someone with these kind of qualities: strong, efficient, eye contact, easy to be with, surprising, normal, wanting opinions, media friendly, informative, keen, representing the organisation, person of the people, expert, humorous, in control.

TK Comprehensive list, perhaps a shade ambitious for a one-off event?

RL Three-off. Anyway, you know what I'm like.

TK Some. Out of this list 'normal' is the only one that strikes a chord.

RL The list isn't about me, it's about the chair.

TK Is it? Nothing aspirational here by any chance? Go on, justify yourself.

RL Right. Clearly you could identify these qualities with a good chair of meetings, a professional chair. But when I'd fully absorbed 'be prepared to be anarchic' and 'make a movie' these actually felt more important than this list.

TK Aha. And why might this be?

RL I guess I was hovering over this imaginary line between art and work, and at the last minute I shifted more towards art, simple as that.

TK I wonder why it took you so long?

RL How do you mean?

TK You really want me to tell you? Well ... it's seemed to me for some time that the art was getting subsumed in a kind of 'correctness' that I find dishonest. By trying so hard to hit the right note of imaginary customer satisfaction, you get lost in that particular detail. This was an artwork after all.

RL Yes and no. It was hovering, like I said.

TK No, you said you were hovering.

RL It's the same thing.

TK Is it?

RL Are you being pedantic?

TK I'm making a point, Richard. This 'hovering' you talk about is pretty airy stuff. It's time to be either more specific or less specific, or just accept that it was a performance piece. Think about it. So, give me some anecdotes.

RL OK, the purchases to start with. The prize, or gift, usually welcome, represents the unexpected, the reward, the irrational stroke, and can cut through British reserve.

TK If you say so. Go on.

RL West Bromwich High Street on Saturday morning was a nugget of gift opportunities. Raffle tickets, England flags and flowery hair clips for the 2pm and the 3pm meetings. Potted polyanthas, rolled green bin bags and an impressive Savoy cabbage for the 4pm meeting. I decided the cabbage should sit beside me next to the chairman's hammer.
Some random fragments:

- 'special guests' are all around you
- reciting the 100 year roll call of mayors
- playing the grand piano
- throwing biscuits at the largest group, on request
- Dennis continually sound-mixing for three hours, whether his volume was up or down
- the lurid décor

- the people who didn't want to leave

Have I answered your question?

TK Sort of.

RL And what did you think of them then, Tania, these three public meetings?

TK I agree with some of what you've said. But there's no need to even refer to this line between the 'performed' and the 'everyday'. I understand why you're doing this analysis-after-the-event and before-the-event stuff, but sometimes I wish you'd just get on and do your thing. At the last minute, this almost happened here. This piece seemed to relate to your work in industry, which you weren't so precious about, so far as I can tell. I think your need for finding a framework, a context, a strategy, is a kind of justification. Who needs it? Just do it, I say. But do it with full-on conviction and people can see it. They're not stupid.

RL What do you get from our relationship, Tania?

TK I'm finding out. But it's all material for me.

23 OCTOBER 03
PERTH, AUSTRALIA

RL Were you OK with all that, Tania?

TK Told you it was risky asking someone else to be me.
Burnt your digits on this one close range, direct hit.
Don't fuck with me I am the business in hand.

16 OCTOBER 03
PERTH, AUSTRALIA

TK So what's this about getting someone to be me in your performance?

RL I thought it could work.

TK What do you mean? Who is she, anyway?

RL I'm going to talk about you, Tania, in the performance. And I thought it would add a dimension to your presence if I talk to Rosie as if she's you.

TK Who's Rosie?

RL I made an audio piece with Rosie Dennis in Wagga Wagga last month. Wasn't entirely happy with it. Now she's coming out to Perth to do this spoken sequence with me, live. I don't think we'll end up using the pre-recorded material though.

TK Does she know you want her to be me?

RL Kind of, I mentioned it in an email. I don't know how she'll feel about it.

TK She can't actually be me.

RL No, but she can symbolise or personify you.

TK Don't try and get clever with me, Richard, I've got my reputation to think of, and a show coming up in Stuttgart in a couple of weeks. She's not even a visual artist. You'll have to make it clear that she's not really me or I'm not agreeing to this.

RL OK.

TK Anyway, does she look like me? And how old is she?

RL She doesn't look like you and I think she's a bit older than you.

TK Is she attractive?

RL Yes, but you're in a league of your own.

TK Piss off. Would I like her?

RL I think you'd get along pretty well.

TK Can you mention my show in your programme notes?

RL Yes.

TK If you want my advice on your performance then you'd better move quickly. Today or tomorrow. After that I'm flat out.

RL Thanks, I'll be in touch.

9 OCTOBER 03
SYDNEY, AUSTRALIA

RL I'm a bit confused, overwhelmed, retracing my parents' steps of late-in-years emigration over here, while I rested not so easy at The Slade.

TK You were confused in Wagga, nothing new in that. You ready for some general responses to the last few weeks?

RL From you?

TK Who else is in the frame?

RL Sure.

TK Is this family history stuff so interesting? You move OK but I wouldn't call it dancing. I want your stuff, not the audience's. Bring it on. Your country needs you. I want the moment. Teach me something, don't confuse me just for the hell of it. Or cram it all in. Be still. Move me, don't be trash. Age is irrelevant, present tense. Take your time.

27 SEPTEMBER 03
WAGGA WAGGA, AUSTRALIA

RL What was your take on the day at large?

TK Someone is looking for a severed kangaroo head. Road over bridge no traffic. Think video. Bad behaviour in the mall eatery and the authorities make their own mistakes. High tech no public in the artist talks at the art gallery. But it gets you thinking about edges softened as corporate man subsumed you more... and the love thing... and real investment.

4 APRIL 02
COLCHESTER, ESSEX

RL How's it going, Tania? Do you want some text printed and displayed on your work table? Shall I organise it for you?

TK As you know I don't normally agree to these 'open studio' things. I'm trying to make sense of it, make the work for myself. The gallery context helps. Here's my statement. Can you leave it on the chair?
I'll be out for a while:
This is my space.
Here is my work.
I don't often open my doors.
I'm not giving everything away.
There's a book on the table called Tania's Ideas Book.
You can make suggestions to me in there.
I may use them. I may not.

AFTERWORD

Responding to a commission from the Firstsite gallery in Colchester to create an installation that would 'reveal artists' practices', Richard Layzell invented a group of four artists and made their work for them. In this way Layzell deconstructed the creative process through the creative process, a kind of making while being detached. Back in his studio after the exhibition had closed, Layzell found himself missing the method and ease of producing the work of one in particular of those four invented artists: Tania Koswycz. He decided to continue fabricating work as Tania. This process gave rise to a relationship of creative provocation in which Richard and Tania sparked each other precisely because they had differing points of view. Richard would ask Tania what she thought about something and found her advice useful. These 'process' conversations eventually became an integral part of Layzell's 'product'. In performances Richard began to speak directly to Tania, later their conversations were published.

One of the solutions that Layzell found to answer the challenge of making artistic decisions was to dramatise his creative thought through the creation of a dialogue with an invented collaborator. It is, after all, often much easier to give advice to others than to oneself. As a mentor to artists, this is something Layzell knows well and perhaps Tania is born out of the need for the type of artistic interlocutor that Layzell is himself, to so many others. His dialogue with Tania gives us a glimpse of the working life of an artist. Sometimes it is humorous and poetic, sometimes esoteric, often refreshingly banal – enabling us to see the role of the artist as one constrained by diurnal practicalities, rather than some mystical process of divine inspiration.

But Tania is more than a foil to bounce ideas off and these dialogues are more than an account of an artistic process. She has enabled the possibility for the everyday to become art; a world where a flat tyre emerges as *The Day of the Moped*. She has become the very stuff which the decision making process he engineered was set up to answer. Which is to say, they have become the artwork.

Joshua Sofaer
New York, January 2008

INDEX

ACKNOWLEDGEMENTS

TK & RL would like to thank: Christopher Bannerman, Philippa Barr, Caroline Bergvall, Daniel Brine, Laura Eldret, Ron Henocq, Lois Keidan, Tom Kelly, Alistair Maclennan, Nikki Millican, Adrian Rifkin, Time Place Space (Australia), Jeni Walwin, and Andy Whall

COLOPHON

Cream Pages was designed and typeset in Futura and E&F Swift by Phil Baines, and printed in the UK by Ripping Image